Oddly Beautiful

Oddly Beautiful

poems by Madelyne Camrud

American Poetry Series

Cover design by Daniel A. Shudlick
Cover art by Madelyne Camrud
Cover art photo by Halo Camrud
Author photo by Jodi Smith
Interior design by Richard D. Natale

The publication of *Oddly Beautiful* is made possible by the generous support of the McKnight Foundation and other contributors to New Rivers Press.

For academic permission or copyright clearance please contact Frederick T. Courtright at 570-839-7477 or permdude@eclipse.net.

New Rivers Press is a nonprofit literary press associated with Minnesota State University Moorhead.

Alan Davis, Co-Director and Senior Editor
Suzzanne Kelley, Co-Director and Managing Editor
Wayne Gudmundson, Consultant
Allen Sheets, Art Director
Thom Tammaro, Poetry Editor
Kevin Carollo, MVP Poetry Coordinator

Publishing Interns:
Katie Baker, Hayley Burdett, Katelin Hansen, Richard D. Natale, Emilee Ruhland, Daniel A. Shudlick

Oddly Beautiful Book Team:
Naomi Nix, Andrew Mendelsohn, Sydney Gill

New Rivers Press
c/o MSUM
1104 7th Avenue South
Moorhead, MN 56563
newriverspress.com

For my husband, Ted,
in memoriam

The birds of night peck at the first stars
that flash like my soul when I love you.

The night gallops on its shadowy mare
shedding blue tassels over the land.

—Pablo Neruda
trans. W. S. Merwin

It is the beauty of the world that makes us more conscious of death, not
the consciousness of death that makes the world more beautiful.

—Christian Wiman
"Notes on Poetry and Religion"
Ambition and Survival: BECOMING A POET

Contents

Part Three

Part One

Because I Can't Forget How It Was

Mornings I rush to the window,
and I don't know if I want to keep it coming
or stop it—I'm speaking of light,
how it begins, breaks the blue wash

we call dawning. But this is not only about light

I try to catch or hold. It's more about failing,
never finding what I've rushed to see.
It's about not even knowing everything washes
white in the end, leaves only blue shadows.

How It Begins

Winter is endless when you're in it, long cold stays,
blue snow stretches every direction.

You head out for groceries in a thick coat,
and find the store is not there.

You spend the night making hot tea you never drink.
Carelessness got you here; you didn't prepare.

You've forgotten, in spite of everything,
you were too caught up in living.

It happened slowly like a marriage unwinding comfortably,
staying inside, turning on fires with a remote.

Try as you might you can't get back that last summer,
nothing can change the Arctic water

that separates you like an animal on an ice floe.
Now the long nights grow longer. You like them for their sleep,

the dreams with slippery hands, one with a man who tossed
a little girl repeatedly into the air,

caught her before that last time when he missed.

The Pulse

Someday one of us will look back
to this, the rain outside the glass,

the two of us under the covers.
One will look back to warm arms, kisses,

but will not get the moment back,
not the way it is now.

It will be like this morning's dream,
close in my mind, but gone. Someday,

after death has come singing between us,
one of us will try to recapture

the smells we know now. One will remember
the rain, how it came before we heard it

and we awoke knowing only its sound
on the pane, listened closely

as a bride in her chamber for her husband.
One of us, eyes closed, will try hard

to see the other, to remember arms,
legs enmeshed, our breaths together,

hearts beating three, four, five, six,
and the two of us, like rain on the glass,

falling deeper into the singing.

Red Pedal Pushers

If you'd not cruised in with the confidence
of one who knew the rules,
red Chevy Bel Air, top down,
that summer I was sixteen
desperate to make something happen.
If you'd not stopped near the dam
and dared me to cross like a high wire walker.

If my friend and I hadn't been walking
in Woodland Park that Sunday afternoon,
had you not stopped to talk.
If I'd not smiled the way I smiled
when I didn't know what to say,
my thighs ripe in pedal pushers,
gray string tied at the knee.

Had the water inside me not begun
its flow that day, ending the next summer
in a rush I couldn't stop—
water spilling over the rocks
that dammed it, a river flowing to another.
In the dapple of light and shade
it was easy to blur choices, let them pass.

A Simple Dance

Because someone doused
the lights

and you kissed me
that night

at the Saturday dance,
your smile

like neon lighting
the dance floor,

your body
a glove, me the hand,

as we moved
to the dance, the dance

so slow, so easy,
because

I had only to count,
one two three,

and let the dance take me
a direction

I hadn't planned,
never bothering

to learn the steps,
because

I knew only
to dance.

First Thing in the Morning, What You Hear

A man is knocking at the door.
Who is he?

I don't know.
Does he come into the house?

No, he only knocks.
Why not invite him in? He could have coffee with us.

He makes me nervous.
There is no need to worry.

Are you sure?
He might take you by the hand if you let him—
he might be your friend.

A man is knocking at the door.
A man is knocking.

This Winter Worse than Most

At night I awaken and listen
to the house creak, its boards sharpening

in the cold. Days we stay inside,
looking out the window,

and wonder at a world so deep
into temperature. A nuthatch

tweaks thistle seed from a feeder
suction-cupped to the pane.

In moments like this spent close to glass,
how understandable my life is,

inside the heavy ribs of my navy sweater.
I watch the small bird rise

and light on a high branch.

The Way It Is

Friends say you are changing and I just keep walking,
moving ahead in the way I always have,

you the rock beside the road. At a crossing,
you don't know where to go.

I don't understand *early cognitive disorder.* Had the doctor
been more compassionate, pulled back

from his computer, looked us in the face.
Could be anything, I insist.

What lies ahead no one knows.

Dread rising inside me like water in ditches —
the words slip from him as easily as ribbons fingered in the wind,

I'd guess Alzheimer's disease.
The river climbs again in our backyard, flooding our house,

washing it away, all roads become one—
a tundra, like the map I dreamed,

no roads, no cities, not even a country. In a world
you can't spell backwards, tipped

farther on its axis, we go out like lambs, and look
everywhere for a cure, seeing only

the rock beginning to tumble, falling deeper.

Walking the Amble Grove

I stumble over logs, moss-covered,
half gone from decay, and imagine

I'm in the thick of your brain.
On a hunt without a gun,

I crisscross broken branches
and forget where I am going.

You lose track of what to say.
This day, like all your days now,

I struggle between trees, rotting
trunks like thoughts breaking off,

and falling. The clearing a half-mile away,
I'm looking, always looking,

the way you look for that long-legged
wild creature running free,

love in its eyes as strong as fear,
neither it, nor us, sure what we'll see

before we reach the end of the grove.

Saturday Morning

My hand strokes your shoulder,
knows your skin in ways
it hasn't yet learned, examines the freckles
you've earned from seasons

we've traversed. In the quiet of our room
I see us young again, a couple
who never got enough of touching.
Sunday afternoon, after riding or walking,
we'd lie on a quilt close to earth,
reaching, stroking through muscle,
flesh. Now in our bed, there is only

this small touch. My hand relaxes
on your shoulder, then moves up to find
my other hand coming around
your neck. I take it for a minute and discover
my own texture: the length of my fingers,
the lines around my knuckles
and nails. Then I let it go, let my hand fall
past your ear, back to your shoulder,
to flesh older than I remember, to your smell,
familiar, your warmth, always new.

Grass

If for one summer we might set the mower
                aside, and let
                        the grass

grow wild as the woodbine on my roof,
                perhaps this love
                        I have

for texture might be satisfied. And if,
                that same summer,
                        I asked

you to lie beside me, and if I took you
                through my knees
                        each

morning and evening, to once again
                make babies, and
                        do it

this time, so intentionally, taking such care
                in the placement
                        of seed—

if we could just lie there, between loving,
                watching the grass
                        grow, never

forgetting the earth, its rich darkness, we might
                become like the grass,
                        and this

sadness—this terrible desire I have to touch
                all that I see
                would be over.

Animal

How ridiculous we've become,
me chasing you

around the house, up and
down the stairs, 2 a.m.,

urinal in my hand,
you having forgotten

we've moved our bedroom
to the main floor.

The night's been one
of interrupted sleep, not a night

for good dreams, not even
a night for shadows

that pick and poke
at the person I don't want to be.

Tonight, I am the shadow,
picking, poking at you

from the side of me
I don't even want to know.

You, the hungry bear,
claw at me.

I, the hunter, fight back,
the urge in my groin

no longer there, having
forgotten love—

my best weapon.

Into the Night

I hear the door open the way you've opened it before
to look out at the weather, hear this time

it does not close, so I run from the kitchen, run
calling your name and, hearing no answer, grab my coat.

I do not see you, 'til past the trees, see you've already
crossed the street, walking on ice away from me,

half-stumbling, fast as you can past neighbors' houses,
not answering my call. And I know as I've been warned,

you, too, can run away. Faster and faster you go, close to falling,
'til I catch up, grab your arm, and plead *Come back!*

We struggle for a minute, my face close, you glaring at me
as if I were a stranger, pulling from my grip until I persuade you,

too cold with no jacket—you give in, and we walk home,
your arm in mine. I know now you could have frozen

like others who've run out into the night, a woman
found in a field last week. I know now I am your keeper,

first time you run into the night, into the cold like a wolf
on the prowl, howling to get back all that you have lost.

Colors Swirl in a Mix of Forgetting

The doctor sends you into a room.
A nurse fires words as if they
were marbles shot with thumb and finger,
in and out of your cranium, one
after the other, cold, hard, direct.

You have no defense.
Listening outside the door, I pray
for days you still talk, understand me.
My shooter clicks, clacks,

thumb to finger, sends words
into your circle, rolling them
as if to make a difference.
The door between us closed.

You struggle for words that won't roll,
those that miss the mark.
Zing, zing, no name for this,
can't finish the sentence.
I imagine kneeling beside you.

We tweak our fingers, shooting,
shooting, missing, missing.
Our fingers ache, thumbnails break
for marbles, beautiful as they roll,
glass smoothed nearly to nothing.

At Marymount

If the sisters tucked our names into the prayer rack
as they said, though you'll not be cured,
I believe their prayers may ease us
as we wait for change, whatever change might be—
you with no headache, a good night's sleep,

and if at Vespers, chapel bells
like light crossing water, God hears
the sisters' voices, words they know by heart,
mine joining in the rising,
Anno Dominus, Magnificat—
if then He smiles down and offers us a blessing;
if I close the song book, and listen,
the sweet falsetto lingering,

God's presence like a pistol shot—
I might come to accept what we have to live with:
train ride, whistle blowing, taking you over
a trestle, a tangle of old wood underneath, and the lake
below deep, far deeper than any we've known.

Evening

The sun's long red tail crosses the lake,
slips easily below the far shore. Now

you call on the cell. The moon rises
behind the east trees. I hear your voice,

I miss you.

Last night the dream about Jesus,
come like a lover, lying on a cot.
I kissed his long, lean body, his gleaming feet.

Tonight, ripples silver the lake's darkness.

I scan the skies. Those who study them
say some sign of water, the smallest
dirt particle would be a miracle on Mars.

The moon half-full—two days, and I'll be home.

Mars won't come around for another
sixty-thousand years, you and I,
by then, like planets released from orbit.

I watch a star fall and spin out to meet the sun.

New life can form without touching the ground.
If all goes well, the sun will rise tomorrow.
I close the blinds and say good night.

The moon slips behind clouds.

Part Two

The Day after Valentine's

In late-afternoon traffic a balloon,
like a heart blown in from somewhere,
crosses the street in front of our car.
I want to stop, run after it, at least turn
for a last look as it passes behind us.
But I am the driver now, you, my passenger,
we travel one way. I follow our lane
at a safe speed, stopping for one red light.

The heart floats farther into the distance,
the string a hand once held, trailing,
still attached. I try hard not to look back.
There's little we can say or do,
cannot retrieve what is lost.

The errant heart drifts aimlessly.

A White Ring Around the Moon

The radio warning fifty degrees below zero,
we're tuned to news: bats in Vermont found frozen
in the snow, noses ringed white, a symptom
of whatever it was that wiped them out.
They forgot the way to their caves like bees
in Texas that forgot their hives. A keeper told me
last summer they wandered aimlessly over clover
like lost jet pilots, as if something in the universe
had changed their radar. And you, love,
                             loose in clover

or out in the cold, would not find your way home—
I know this. Once you ran out, didn't come back
when I called, brushed me off like a mosquito
when I caught up. But, tonight, unlike bees and bats,
we cohabit in ways they cannot. Warmed by a heat vent,
not working as hard for good, we are just hanging around,
                                  under the moon,
its ring a sign the cold will stay a long time.

Your Body Still Here

Snow all morning through the trees,
falling past the deck railing.
I sit staring out the window,
brush snow aside and try to write.

The phone rings once, twice.
When I answer, no one is there.
You come from our bed
looking like a ghost
in your white shorts, t-shirt.
It was no one, I say,
then help you back to bed,
you the one I grieve, your body
still here, parts of you missing, gone.
Already the table is heaped white.

I push the pen through
all that has fallen.
There is no other way.
It is cold work. I can tell
the snow will fall a long time.

A Painting Affair

You said our life would be easy,
the canvas blank, filled with promise.

You were always the one, said
nothing matters but love, the right colors.

I spent years looking for bouquets,
pink, yellow, coral, and white—

my way of saying *No*. And the leaves,
oh yes, the leaves, how I twisted,

curled them from stems, hairs of my brush
blending, stroking what has drawn me

from your side all these years. This morning
on tiptoe, I sneak downstairs and leave you sleeping.

I leave you for horses on an easel,
horses waiting for the right blue, a wash of white.

Horses I can't finish, horses running
as if there is no right or wrong, running to escape

in color after color I lay down.

Bridges

We slap leather, like horses steaming down strange roads,
heading for bridges. Blinded,

we are a runaway team pulling a make-shift wooden cart,
skids scraping gravel, singletree

clattering like bridge boards, wagons rattling across.

Harnessed, we stay with the gallop until the hitching pole
drops, hits the road,

the cart tips sideways. That day you pulled me to the cul-de-sac
and back, gripping my wrist,

I could not release your hold. Didn't want us to be this team,
you stumbling as if spavined,

leading me, hitched. Didn't know where you were taking me
until on our neighbor's lawn—

like a colt let out to pasture, knees lifting to your chest,
hooves digging turf, you ran

unbroken that long minute, crossing one bridge, then another.

Sketches

Last night
you looked in the mirror,
asked *Who is he?*

At breakfast, I grab a large orange
and shave its peelings off in spirals.

I break it into sections, and the whole
world collapses in my hand.

How do the grieving grieve?

Are we no different from the trees,
washed in wind and rain?

All morning rain is falling.
I crank the window open,
poke my head out to listen. Just then
a bird breaks into song, its voice
like a spoon striking a glass rim.

In the window box below me
a new red flower has opened, petals
looping from a center, ready, wet.

Amaryllis in a White Pot

I wake early and rush downstairs,
to check the thick, bold stalk,
rising from black soil as eagerly as a penis
      for lovemaking.

                After months,
a dark closet, the red bud begins to open.
Snowmelt below the hill, coulee
flows to the river we call Red.

Oh, what joy!
All desire narrowed down to one.

Sundowning

Shuffling, stumbling one room to another,
you're like a ship gone off-course in rough water

until, for some reason, stopped, head down thinking,
you are a storm spent in our kitchen. I come up

to you and wrap my arms around your neck.
I lay my cheek on yours, pressing my body close,

and the business card you took from the coat check
this morning, all evening in your hand, falls from your fingers.

You jumble out words I don't understand, but I can tell
they are romantic. I think of us like this, dark hallway, kisses

we couldn't stop. You kept asking between breaths,
See you tomorrow night? I whispered, *Yes,*

then you left. My body ached, aches now. Here,
near an island, but here is where we are,

in from wind and weather, caught in a dead calm.

Longing for What Is Not

You   caught up   in dreams,   snoring   like a small drum.
I lie beside you,
listening.

Our dim bedroom,   all other sound come to nothing   I imagine us
at the bottom,
a thick forest.

Moss grows over   our arms   legs   faces—   moist dirt
cooling
our damp skin.

Dressing gown   fallen   from my shoulders,   I sink deeper,
melting
like snow in rain—

you come to me   in secret   not knowing   what to say.
I whisper
what no one else

will ever hear.   Slowly I give up   my pleasure,   fingertips squeezing out
those lovely
unsung notes.

I am   a hundred   open lips   craving   your one long stem.

What Has Fallen

The garden has lost its luster and I have risen early.

Last night, a strong wind snapped twigs,
sent branches across the lawn.

I stand in the doorway, wanting to go
back in time, more careful for order.

This morning's small breeze lifts
begonia blossoms from the sidewalk.

Not long now until autumn, soon I'll cut and haul
garden stems to the compost bin for winter.

In your leather chair you wait for the day.

The hibiscus topiary has fallen on the deck.
I go out in a hurry and set it straight.

A rabbit hunches low under the global arborvitae.

Foraging

In this bed where we once made love,
limbs supple, willing,

I lie, eyes half-closed, watching you pace
the floor like an animal caged.

Worn from a night of little sleep, cleaning
the bathroom, changing sheets,

I'm as useless as the leaves, trees smoldering
like ash, burned for winter.

You forage dresser drawers as if you were a bear
searching for honey he can't find.

The sky as gray as porridge this late October,
a last red leaf, tip of the maple,

holds on by one small stem. Flesh,
blood joined by chance

cannot be taken back. This morning
I don't want to leave

the comforter I'm under, don't want to trek
downstairs for breakfast.

I know you need my care,
but I'm no more than prey, lying here,

half-eaten, dragged home.

Marriage Bed

> You made your bed, now lie in it.
>
> —Mother wrote me after our elopement.

Don't want to lie in this bed I made,
don't want to make it—want to forget
the lines we crossed years ago.
Jammed against the wall in a space
not meant for sleeping, you
crosswise, end of the bed, fallen
in your after-pill stupor, I cross again,
chasing shadows: Mother caring for Father,
skeletal, cancerous in their bedroom;
Grandmother hushing seven children,
her husband dying a long year
on the sofa, tuberculosis.

From this bed no longer sacred,
I watch shadows from fan blades
crossing the ceiling like legs of spiders
crawling to the corners where all the mothers,
wives have come, lured by their own shadows.

Who's to say when the tenderness leaves?

Three times vowing *in sickness and in health*,
I stay the course for what I glimpsed
through blinds this morning, the lawn
green under an inch of April snow.

Shaving You

After nicks and cuts, bleeding I couldn't stop,
I went to Kohl's, bought an electric,
the kind you—and my father who used

a straight edge, brushed soap in a cup—
never liked. Dad was a lather and razor guy,
you, an aerosol can, Gillette razor man.

Foamed up like Santa Claus, you
teased me for kisses in those early years.
I ran from you though I liked

your baby-bottom cheek we won't get
with this triple sickle gadget
circling the contours of your face like a street cleaner.

I shake whiskers from the cutters into the sink—
as if I were emptying a lawn bag
after mowing, flakes of your skin mixed in,

imagined plaque, thin as hair, shorn from your brain.

In the Bathroom

When the rich amber liquid rises in the urinal,
I lean close and listen, the pressure
of its flow like steam from a geyser.

Holding the warm plastic, I take in an odor,
acrid, oddly pleasing, a stream seeping from the caves,
rocks, and caverns in your pelvis. Emptied,

flushed the color of sky just after a sunset,
the contents swirl to the sewer. I whisper,
You've done well. Sometimes you say, *Thank you.*

Still Life

On our bed I lie searching
for something more than stillness.

The only motion in the room
is fan blades whirring,

ceiling's center. The sun's rays
come wheeling through the east panes,

casting light pure as honey,
on papered walls.

I want to be more than this,
my body as empty as the mirror

hanging high over the bed;
the filigree of its frame

cracked and aging. I want to hear
again the trees, the way

they whispered when I was young.
But there is only the fern

spilling from white ceramic
on the stand in the corner,

a band of gold its base,
like the ring on the hand

that rests beside me
on the sheet, all that I see

of a life, quietly breathing.

Turning

That day in the bathroom when your feet refused to move
as if in an ice block, I didn't know where to turn.

We carried you to the car. ER nurses wheeled you,
lifted you on a mat, plopped you onto a bed.

An hour later, you walked the halls, half-skipping,
winking at nurses but, roped in by a rule,

we couldn't be released that late in the day. Couldn't
escape the helpers coming in, checking what

they didn't need to check. You kept climbing over
the bed rails—and me trying to sleep on a miserable cot.

All that long night, I imagined you, another night,
the one we met. You wielding a bat, the fast pitch,

ball out of the park, stands wracked with applause,
you rounding the bases, sprinting home.

The Snow Turns Blue

I knew it was coming, always does—
but oh, how things have changed
under the weight of it,
having to scrape or shovel it up.

Before the snow came,
I thought we'd grow old together
like taking a slow walk
downhill. Instead,
I'm coasting alone
like a child on a sled,
looking back over my shoulder,
sorry for all I've left behind,
afraid of what lies ahead.

Small Bird Fallen

A bird lies panting below the evergreen.
Snow around the house, temperature
cold, I pace from one window
to another in my white robe, bare feet.
I want the bird inside, want to heal it;
but I am dealing with oatmeal you don't want.
I make toast and you tell me you want to sleep.

You cross the hardwood floor in one slipper,
one shoe, and hold your head as if
holding a wound to stop the bleeding.

                    Each day
I try to help you, but today a sinking feeling
overtakes me. Scraping away
what you've not eaten, stacking
the dishwasher, even before I look out
I know the bird has grown quiet in the snow.

Ice crystals blow like ash over its body.

Vipassana

Having sat, letting
my thoughts pass
like a breath, in,
then out, I open
my eyes to this room,
its objects so still:
the bed with a quilt,
a chair drawn close,
the table with a lamp,
a figurine, its large skirt
hollowed out for a plant.
Their stillness is like a glass
half-filled with water,
a transience to see through,
a romance that I have,
not for the chair, the bed,
or the table as they are,
but rather for what they were,
for where I've been, how close
to nothing, and how blessed.

Part Three

Weekend at the Lake

From the dock, we watch two gulls,
out on the water. One lifts its wings
and leaves the other floating.

You take the Swedish saw,
cut sapling popple on the back lot.
I hack willow for a basket.

Yesterday, the doctor let us know
an odd blessing: you are still
in early stages, we have time remaining.

No one can say how long before
you'll turn from me like a stranger.

You push the squeaky reel mower
and work up a sweat trimming
clump birch. Toward evening

we look out again over the water.
One gull waiting.

Running

It's become plain in every muscle,
the deepest matter of my brain,

I'm on a dead run. You walk
long, dark halls, empty places.

I never stop to face your eyes,
the way you look at me, pleading,

the light that once guided me,
gone dim. Yesterday,

you were the man in an album,
photographs, newspaper

stories, clipped now, pasted in—
nothing simple about any of this.

How long since evenings we walked
gravel roads. Purple clouds,

rows of willow leafless, golden,
a red sun. We walked slowly,

no reason in the world to run.

Retreat

After five years of war, it comes to me clearly
at the supper table, having to

cut up your meat, potatoes, and green beans.

You speak garbled language I don't understand,
grab your head and say it aches.

You don't want to eat. This time not the first time,
but this is when it hits me, how long

we've fought, and how hard, not even to make headway,
but to simply hold the line. Like a soldier

meeting the enemy, face to face, first time,
I recognize weapons stronger than yours or mine.

A deserter, I clear the table, abandoning our last bastion.

The Way You Leave

1.

In the laundry room
I secretly pack your suitcase.
I write your name indelibly
on jeans, shirts, underwear,
then drive you, these clothes,
two pair of shoes down the road.
I drive as handily as one
drives from a crime,
clean getaway.

2.

A CNA, the RN, and I scuttle in
small parts of your life behind your back,

speed them on a cart: your photograph,
family pictures, framed biography.

Then I walk out and leave you, not
telling you I'll be back, not even saying

I am going. Like Lot's wife, I look back once,
a pillar of salt, wanting to go in,

give you a hug, but I believe
they know better, the nurse, the aides, a director—

Better not say good-bye, would only make it harder.

Is the Eve in me biting the apple—
their tempting words the serpent?

This can be yours; you deserve it.

I take the easy road through the door
locked to keep you, hearing their whispers:

Don't make it harder for him. Go to the lake, take it easy.

3.

First night in our house.
Like the moment after one fires a shot,
the awful silence never stops. Emptiness everywhere,
our thousands of days, countless hours

stripped bare. I look around the rooms
not yet recalling the dream: you smiling
behind a glass wall. I struggled to release you.

My stomach as if ground to gunpowder
reminds me that you, the husband, will never
again be in this house with me, the wife.

4.

I clean the lake cabin the way
Mother did laundry,
ringer washer, morning Dad died.

I phone the nurse, How is he?
He's pacing the floor,
won't sit unless I sit with him.
How'd you keep him home so long?

Would it be all right if I talk to him?
No, I don't think so. Only make it worse.

A hundred miles away, I sleep well each night,
Stay a week; get the rest you deserve.

The voices in my heart quiet as stones.

5.

You, a zombie on the couch,
don't know I am with you. I hold you
like dead wood in my arms.
A week ago I brought you here.
Now you slip from my arms.
I cannot stop you, couch to carpet
like a body down a riverbank,
drowning. I call the CNAs.
Three come quickly, cannot wake,
cannot lift you from whatever
has pulled you down, left you sinking.
I cannot turn against the current.
He hasn't yet made the adjustment,
the director urges, *Give him more time.*

6.

One week gone, half another,
you're resigned to die.

I see it in your eyes.

I wheel you into the courtyard,
sit on a bench beside you.

Hedges all around,
cotoneaster, huckleberry—

and roses, bushes of roses.
I ask if you see them.

It is June. Your eyes
are empty.

I chatter. You say nothing.

Your Husband Is Not Responding

they call to tell me
you've gone beyond their care
have to take you somewhere
and I say *home then*
home on hospice
find a driver who ramps
you into a van
straps you in a wheelchair
while I hold you close
as we cross the river
driver one hand on the wheel
phone in the other has worked us in
a woman on the line
low on oxygen
pleading the driver to come
part of me wanting
to say *Let's go to that woman*
she may have more time
another part knowing
I want you home to die
as the driver careens
around corners to our house
our son and his friends
waiting on the driveway
to carry you up the steps
down the hall to the den
where we slept those last months
home to make ready
for that other long journey

Close to Summer Solstice

Praise the bats alive in caves, wings folded like sleeping angels.
Praise the bees flown home safely to creamy combs.

Praise because there is no reason to praise—
you barely breathing, stopped eating.

Praise the wren sending a song from the roof of her house.
A diva on stage, she feeds all those hungry voices,

babies anxious, like you, like me,
to burst their skin and grow feathers.

Praise the vine kept in for winter, set out again
this summer, stronger than ever.

Praise the lives we've planted. Praise the garden
that blooms as if you are not dying.

Praise the first fly flown through my window
this unscreened spring—its darkness a sure thing,

never been more true. You are leaving me.
Praise the stars, the moon.

Praise Him who turns the earth, the planets, and the years.
Soon we will have passed the longest day.

Leaving

I moisten your lips, try to tickle a smile,
turn on the light inside you, a body winged,
waiting, pinned like the butterfly inside
my window, clouds ominous in the glass.
Nothing to do but watch you dying
three days in our den, hospice sheets,
pillows protecting your arms from metal railings.
Legs astonishingly slim: long femur,
tibia, fibula, angling down to feet, bones
piercing the sheet. I press my ear to your chest.
Breath nearly lost in the cavern of your rib cage,
a heart still beating against the glass
like the white wings, their small black dots
looking like hearts in my clumsy imperfect hands.
I laid them, fragile, a lamp's mantel near the window.

The last morning I leave your bedside
and take a chair, not yet believing you will leave
as easily as you do, not even hearing
your last breath until I do not hear the next,
not seeing the room fill with sunshine,
the unfolding, you lifting,
wings flitting, one flower to another.

Silence Comes to My Window

Daybreak.
A mini-forest of evergreens

on my deck,
twinkle lights

that will soon
take a message from the timer

and click off. Suddenly
one small bird

sweeps in and sits
on the tip of a tree.

Quiet and brown, plain for sure,
he is a presence,

nonetheless—in feathers,
gentle curves,

delicate feet.

Sketches II

Those last days,
you spoke only my name,
        Madelyne, Madelyne,

looking at me as if you'd been forsaken.
I tucked you into bed. You looked up at me saying,
I love you, I love you, I love you,

as if there were not enough times,
enough ways to say it.

                I gave away your suits, shirts, and neckties.
                Your shoes in the closet gather dust.

From the Jacuzzi, high window,
clouds like milky cheesecloth float
across the clear blue.

I imagine you that way, trailing off, becoming sky.

The Rain Finally Ended

Less than a month since
you were zipped up,
a bag wheeled from our house
like refuse, I gather in
the dead: a warbler hung
on a shrub, a sparrow
fallen on the deck.
I carry them in plastic
like soldiers home in body bags,
thinking of a photo,
morning newspaper,
car bomb survivors
of what in other wars
would have killed them.
Home from Iraq, they pose
in San Antonio, some minus
a hand, an arm, or a leg,
one with no limbs at all.
My body still intact,
as if there never were a war.

What You Left Me

Begin with the dream, the life
that is only a film, black and white, silent.

Then, the awkward contraption I push
down the aisle, a larger than life stroller, no baby in it.

Hard to see in semi-darkness, I squeeze
between front row seats and discover the movie

features you the hero, me unsettled, wanting more—
that's the picture. I want to get up

and scrawl my name across the screen
as if to say this is how it was.

This was us. No one in the theatre but me,
lovers in the last row, gone. I turn and look back,

wanting your arm around my shoulder.
I can't stop gripping the handle

of this crazy quasi-stroller wedged in sideways,
too close. Images flicker across the screen,

a gray blur. The reel unwinds like a clock,
The End repeating again and again

as if the awful truth cannot be said enough.

Evening II

Like autumn sun you went quickly.

Your body slipped back into earth.
A spirit, you dispersed like sparks in wind.

This October not so different from others,
nothing in nature seems to notice you're not here.

The maple still blazes like a firestorm,
burns leaves red, then maroon; bronze mums

flower in pots, kale ruffles deck baskets.
Ducks graze the coulee with usual leisure.

As for me, I've no choice but to grieve,
to turn this sadness like the seasons, working

it like a field before planting. Lord God,
if you hear me, I'd take him home again

any way I could just to have autumn once more
with him at this table watching the ducks

live such happiness—you can see it
in their wake—and us, amazed, as always,

at their steady angle upward, their sure flight.

Our Sleep Is Deep Now

And Baucis noticed her husband was beginning
to put forth leaves, and he saw that she, too,
was producing leaves and bark. They were turning into trees . . .

—Mary Zimmerman,
from *Metamorphosis*, a play.

Memories tucked under our bent limbs,
trapped like butterfly wings,
here—the dreams:

The storm like a drum song over,
we fly to an island, but the plane is too slow.

We drive now past ditches,
water high both sides of the road.
Seeds paired in neat sacks

float past us.

Quiet leaves, a shallow breeze—
feathers of algae floating votive candles.

Water becomes air.
We are under, inside,

over.

We have nowhere to go.

Swim,   swim,
breathe,   breathe.

Our sleep is deep now. Someone else must tend the world.

All things taller—
           rocks, trees,

                    spreading like the wings of the butterfly,

                      transparent,
                              free,

      flown far beyond our closed windows.

We sleep the long night, sleep as if we'll never wake,
and look up to what we once thought was heaven—
                            there a tall tree,

                roots running down to us,
                      deep,

            rings circling back to a center,
                    branches shaking, mingling

           like leaves in strong wind.

We climb higher, the branches our ladder,
      until we can no longer climb.

                    The tree grows taller, piercing the sky.

We come together, the universe in a leaf.

Stepping from the Shower

I wonder if you are watching,
remembering my body, times you soaped
and stroked, entered me so easily.
You no longer here, I close my eyes
and see your thighs, long muscles
hard, erect. I imagine you
no longer desire me, do not miss me
like I miss you. There's no reason
for you to be sorry, not there
in all that light, knowing everything
before, after, and between, even
the flashing blue lights that landed
in a pasture, frightened farmhands
half to death. And those rings left
in wheat fields west of Hatton, no footprints
in or out: what do you make of them?

Sometimes you're at the tip of my mind,
as if you might be trying to answer
all that makes me wonder, the sightings
last night, blue, green lights crossing
the sky—a falling star; a meteor?
Is it possible you could send a sign
like the loud knock that woke me
from a good dream last week?
I want a way to rise higher, a little
closer to you, the mysteries raining
down on this earth, once yours,
cold, wet, toweling my hips.

Scent of a Man

The tin as old as our marriage,
I lift the lid and smell you after a shave,
your cheek as smooth as sweet cream.

This same can in your suitcase,
night of our elopement. In new baby doll pajamas
I watched you shaving, morning after,

not yet believing you'd be mine for a lifetime.

Thank you Colgate-Palmolive for this man
I miss. Can't possibly throw out
this can *for men*—hardbound, handsome,

and young, a genie saved in years of bathrooms,
mine again in one scant whiff of talcum.

Blizzard

I've found you in strange places,
your handkerchief in the freezer,

clean and white behind ice cream,
tucked near boxes of broccoli, frozen peas.

Later, in your wallet, leather worn
to fit your pocket, slid under a plate in the buffet.

I called out *Ted*, worried at first
you'd misplaced it, tried hard to find it,

then laughed, opening the fold,
finding a twenty you'd saved for me.

You come back the way you left,
a little at a time, like crumbs tossed along

a path I follow. In small acts of survival
we all make our way—you stashed

what you could for reasons I can't explain.
This morning, in heavy snowfall,

two small birds pecking suet
in a storm that won't let up,

flakes thicken on the glass.
I'm here with a pen, trying hard

to set down what I know of our lives
as if, someday, someone might find us.

Oddly Beautiful

Heading home from the grocery store,
I am stopped by red letters, large and desperate,
spray-painted on concrete like a warning:

I NEED LOVE.

Then it comes to me: the two of us
under the apple tree, bending a branch
to hang a birdhouse, blossoms falling all around.
In the falling, one petal catches on
the corner of your mouth, and when I touch you there,
through that velvet, your face grows suddenly,
oddly beautiful.

The Bird in My House

A small bird slept in my house last night.
Some may doubt it but I swear
I found him like an oversized moth
fluttering against the glass, kitchen window.
Couldn't shoo him out
though I tried again and again.
The bird, smarter than I, more nimble,
stopped high atop a cupboard I could not reach—
nothing to do but let him roost.

                    The season late,
wind and rain had changed the trees.
If I were a bird, I'd have sought shelter, too.
As it was, I went out for the evening,
and, home again, found the bird nowhere,
a truth that refused to come to light.
Upstairs in bed, I imagined him,
head tucked under a wing, sleeping
the way you rested, head on your arm,
beside me. I turned over and tried to sleep,
but all I could think of was the bird.

                    I wondered again
how he found his way into my house,
come not at all like a thief, more like

whatever it is that breathes love into the night.

Acknowledgements

"The Pulse," "Grass," "Saturday Morning," "Still Life," and "Silence Comes to My Window" were previously published in a chapbook, *The Light We Go After*, Dacotah Territory press, Minnesota State University Moorhead, 2006.

Poems in this collection appeared, sometimes in different versions, in the following journals:

The Alembic: "Grieving"
Descant: "The Day after Valentine's"
Painted Bride Quarterly: "Animal"
Soundings East: "Survivors"
Water~Stone Review: "How Death Begins"
The Merton Seasonal: "Vipassana"
New Millennium Writings: "The Pulse," "The Bird in My House"
WordWrights!: "Grass"

I offer my gratitude to these organizations and publications for their support.

I thank everyone who graciously helped Ted and gave me respite during his illness: our children and their families; extended family; friends and caregivers, especially Carol, who was on constant call, and Linda; and Glenda, a grief counselor. Thanks also to the community that seemed to understand—doors were opened, lines dissolved; prayers and sympathy were generously offered.

For this collection of poems I owe thanks to Barbara Crow, friend and poet, who read the work countless times, and to other poets essential in bringing the work to completion: Mark Vinz, Thom Tammaro, Julie Larson, and Melanie Crow. Special thanks to Susan Meyers who helped "wrap it up."

Thank you to Suzzanne Kelley, Andrew Mendelsohn, and everyone at New Rivers Press for their editing, advice, kind words, and whatever it took to make *Oddly Beautiful* a published work.

I will always be grateful to Jay Meek, my poet mentor. My deepest gratitude goes to Ted, my dear supportive husband of fifty years.

About the Author

Madelyne Camrud has lived all but nine months of her life in North Dakota. She received degrees in visual arts and creative writing at The University of North Dakota. She taught in the English department before taking a position at the North Dakota Museum of Art where she served as director of Audience Development. For several years, Camrud curated the Museum's auctions. Her poems have appeared in numerous journals including *Kalliope*, *Painted Bride Quarterly*, *Descant*, *Soundings East*, *Water~Stone Review*, and in the anthologies *Prairie Volcano* and *The Talking of Hands*. Camrud is the author of *This House Is Filled with Cracks*, a Minnesota Voices Prize winner in poetry published by New Rivers Press in 1994. Two of her poems were chosen to air on Garrison Keillor's *Writers Almanac*. In the spring of 2005, North Dakota Poet Laureate Larry Woiwode named Camrud an Associate Poet Laureate of North Dakota.